FOOTSTEPS TO FREEDOM
THE UNDERGROUND RAILROAD

FAMOUS FIGHTERS

WAYNE L. WILSON

PURPLE TOAD
PUBLISHING

FOOTSTEPS TO
FREEDOM
THE UNDERGROUND RAILROAD

FAMOUS FIGHTERS by Wayne L. Wilson
FREE AT LAST? by Claire O'Neal
THE NEED FOR FLIGHT by Claire O'Neal
GOING UNDERGROUND by Amie Jane Leavitt

PUBLISHER'S NOTE

The *Footsteps to Freedom: The Underground Railroad* series covers slavery and racism in United States history. Some of the events told in this series may be disturbing to young readers. The data in this book has been researched in depth, and to the best of our knowledge is factual. Although every measure is taken to give an accurate account, Purple Toad Publishing makes no warranty of the accuracy of the information and is not liable for damages caused by inaccuracies.

ABOUT THE AUTHOR

Wayne L. Wilson has authored numerous biographical and historical books for children and young adults. He received a Master of Arts in Education with a specialization in Sociology and Anthropology from UCLA. He is also a screenwriter and member of the Writer's Guild of America.

Printing   1   2   3   4   5   6   7   8   9

Publisher's Cataloging-in-Publication Data
Wilson, Wayne L.
  Famous Fighters / written by Wayne L. Wilson.
    p. cm.
Includes bibliographic references and index.
ISBN 9781624692130
1. Underground Railroad--Juvenile literature. 2. Antislavery movements--United States--Juvenile literature. I. Series: Footsteps to Freedom The Underground Railroad.
 E450 2016
 973.7115
Library of Congress Control Number: 2015941830   ebook ISBN: 9781624692147

CONTENTS

INTRODUCTION

The Avenging Angel

John Brown began the war that ended American slavery and made this a free Republic. His zeal in the cause of my race was far greater than mine. I could live for the slave, but he could die for him.[1] —Frederick Douglass

"Blow Ye the Trumpet, Blow!"

John Brown loved this hymn about Gideon, who was chosen by God to free the people of Israel.[2] When the angel of the Lord blows his trumpet, Gideon takes up his sword and is victorious over the enemy. John Brown saw himself as Gideon, an instrument of God's wrath and awakened by God's trumpet to destroy the evils of slavery and punish the men who owned slaves for their sins.

As he closed his eyes, he wondered, Why is there still slavery in 1848?

The hymn played over and over in John Brown's head, and even though he was asleep, he remained upright in his rocking chair, holding an open Bible in his lap and tapping one foot. Suddenly the door flew open and so did his eyes, but they calmed when he saw the young black boy skip in. The child hopped onto his knee.

"Good morning, Mr. Brown! Oh, I'm sorry, were you asleep?" he asked, riding his knee like a horse.

"Me? No . . . I never sleep," Brown replied, half joking. Yawning, he closed his Bible and placed it on the table next to him.

"Then why are your eyes so red?"

4

And indeed they were. His intense gray-blue eyes looked as if they were floating in a pool of blood.

"I haven't slept lately," Brown answered, rubbing his grizzled chin.

"Why?"

Brown gave him a playful bear hug. "Because I've been searching for pesky little boys that need a spanking for asking too many questions!"

The giggling boy wrestled out of Brown's grasp and ran to the open front door.

"Try to catch me, Mr. Brown!"

John Brown smiled. "Noooo . . . you're too fast for me, Mister Lyman Epps, Jr."

"Oh, I almost forgot. My father told me to ask you to come over later so you can make plans to meet some new friends tonight."

"Good. Well, tell Mr. Epps I'll come by after I get a little more rest."

"I thought you said you never sleep?"

"Ooooh, just wait till I get a hold of you!" Brown yelled, jumping up with his arms out. The boy bounded out the door, laughing. Brown followed him onto the porch and into the bright sunlight. Lyman beckoned Brown to chase him as he trotted backwards. Brown shook his head and waved him off as he leaned against the doorjamb. He watched Lyman race down the trail to his neighboring farm.

The smile on Brown's narrow face faded as he remembered how, when he was twelve, he had befriended a slave boy around the same age who was owned by

5

John Brown

the people they visited. The boy was smart and very nice to John. They had a wonderful time playing together. That is, until he saw how the slave master mistreated his friend, making the boy sleep in raggedy clothes in the bitter cold and savagely beating him.[3]

He also recalled a fugitive slave who ran up to him begging for help. Slave catchers were after him. Brown hid him in his cabin, but upon hearing horses galloping toward them, Brown told the man to climb through the window and hide in the bushes. Once the riders were gone, he found the man cowering in terror behind a log.[4]

These are things you never forget, just like in 1837 when Elijah P. Lovejoy, an editor, was killed. He published an antislavery newspaper called *The St. Louis Observer*. He was shot to death protecting his printing press from a proslavery mob.[5]

These and many similar experiences deeply affected John Brown. He declared war on slavery forever and vowed to end this terrible practice of enslaving human beings.

Raised in a very strict and religious family, Brown's parents taught him all people were created equal. Blacks were always welcomed in his home. John and his father, Owen, volunteered for the Underground Railroad. This informal organization guided fugitive slaves through a network of people and hiding places from the South and to freedom in the northern United States or Canada. Volunteers had to be alert at all times.

Brown was exhausted because early that morning he had returned to his farmhouse in New York after escorting fugitive slaves over 250 miles to Canada.[6] For years he had been hiding fugitives and leading five to six people at a time to stations in the North. Tonight he and Lyman, Sr. planned to meet with a new group of runaways that were due to arrive from the South, and they needed to find a safe haven for them.

Brown was proud to live in a community with black families. He'd been warned that it was dangerous for a white family to live among black people, but Brown knew it was possible for blacks and whites to live and work together.

W.E.B. Du Bois once described John Brown as "the man who of all Americans has perhaps come nearest to touching the real souls of black folk. . . . John Brown worked not simply for Black Men—he worked with them; and he was a companion of their daily life, knew their faults and virtues, and felt, as few white Americans have felt, the bitter tragedy of their lot."[7]

Ten years later, John Brown was introduced to a woman he called "one of the bravest persons on this continent."[8] She was equally passionate, tough, fearless, spiritual, and one of the greatest conductors of the Underground Railroad . . . a person Brown fondly nicknamed General Tubman.

On May 9, 1935, a six-ton bronze memorial to famed abolitionist John Brown was unveiled at Lake Placid by his neighbor and friend, Lyman Epps.

CHAPTER 1

Harriet Tubman: The Moses of Her People

The midnight sky and the silent stars have been the witnesses of your devotion to freedom and of your heroism.[1]

—Frederick Douglass to Harriet Tubman

One Saturday night in 1849 the slaves inside their cabin heard Harriet Tubman singing. She often sang hymns and spirituals, but this one stood out. It was a message to her family and friends:

When that old chariot comes
I'm going to leave you,
I'm bound for the Promised Land.
Friends, I'm going to leave you.

She planned to escape—and by morning she was gone.

Her owner, Edward Brodess, had died, and Tubman feared his widow would sell her family to a plantation in the Deep South. Her

Harriet Tubman's courage, faith, and success earned her the name Moses after the biblical person who led the enslaved Israelites out of Egypt to freedom. Whenever she was ready to take people down freedom's road, she'd give them a signal. She might sing a spiritual outside their cabin. She would urge them: "It's time to go North."

brothers were afraid to leave, so she decided to go alone. She believed God chose this time for her to seek freedom. She later said, "There were two things I had a right to . . . liberty or death; if I could not have one, I would have the other."[2]

Tubman hid in the woods during the day and walked by night following the North Star, which led to the free states. A white Quaker woman gave her a paper of introduction, which Harriet gave to another woman at the next house. This was Harriet's first experience with the Underground Railroad, and it taught her the importance of secrecy when traveling from station to station.

At one stop she was given a broom to sweep the yard so people would think she worked there. When she crossed the "magic" line into the free state of Pennsylvania, she joyfully said, "I felt like I was in heaven."[3]

Harriet was born a slave under the name Araminta Ross in Maryland around 1820 to Harriet "Rit" Green and Benjamin Ross. Her parents called her Minty. She became Harriet Tubman after marrying John Tubman and taking her mother's first name.

During childhood, Harriet worked hard and endured severe beatings by her owners. In her teens she tried to protect another slave from an angry overseer. The overseer threw a two-pound lead weight and hit Harriet in the head. It left a scar on her forehead. All her life she was plagued by spells in which she'd black out without notice. She began having visions that she believed were signs from God.

Tubman felt very alone in the North. "I was a stranger in a strange land," she remarked.[4] She swore to return to Maryland and free her family. She found jobs as

Harriet Tubman (far left) in 1887 with family and neighbors at her home in Auburn, New York. From Left to right: Tubman; adopted daughter, Gertie Davis; Harriet's second husband, Nelson Davis; Lee Chaney (a neighbor's child); "Pop" John Alexander (boarder in Tubman's home); Walter Green (neighbor's child); Blind "Aunty" Sarah Parker (boarder); and Dora Stewart (great-niece and granddaughter of Harriet's brother Robert).

a cook and servant in private homes and hotels. She saved her money to go back for them.

Harriet returned to Maryland in 1850 and freed her sister's family. Months later she made the dangerous trip back and rescued her brother and other slaves. On another trip she brought back her parents, who could not walk long distances. An old horse pulled them in a rickety wagon. She tried to rescue her husband, but he had remarried and refused to join her.

Harriet Tubman made nineteen trips to the South and guided more than three hundred slaves to freedom. She once proudly stated: "I was the conductor of the Underground Railroad for eight years . . . and I never ran my train off the track, and I never lost a passenger."[5]

Tubman was a shrewd planner. Slaves didn't work on Sunday mornings, so she would start her train on Saturday nights. This gave the people more time to get

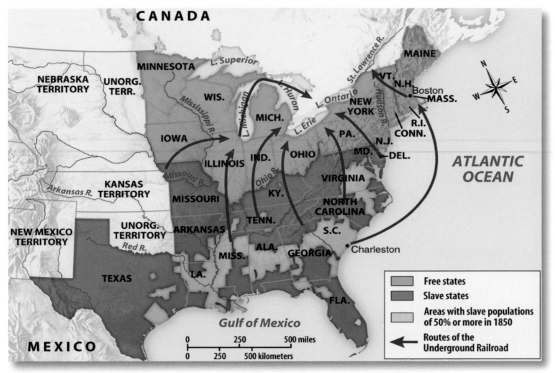

Conductors used many routes to lead slaves to freedom.

away before they were missed. Escapes were often made during the winter on cold, dark nights, when people who might report them were indoors.

The travelers climbed mountains, crossed rivers, and walked through thick forests. If they heard horses, they would hide, sometimes standing in cold and dirty swamps loaded with snakes and alligators.[6]

Harriet pushed her companions hard and never let them lag. Fugitives were often exhausted, with bleeding feet and aching bones. Some wanted to quit and go home, but Harriet wouldn't let them—not if her routes could be revealed. She didn't hesitate to point her pistol at a person, warning: "You go on or die!"[7]

Harriet survived by her wits and her faith in God's protection. She couldn't read, but was crafty. She fooled a group of slave catchers after overhearing them read a wanted poster about Harriet Tubman being illiterate. She pulled out a book and pretended to read. They walked away. Slave owners were so afraid of her, they offered a $40,000 reward for her capture.[8]

The Moses of Her People unselfishly helped others her entire life. William Still wrote of Tubman, "Her like is probable was never known before or since."[9]

Pass Codes and Disguises

Actual railroad terms were used as codes and passwords on the Underground Railroad. "Agents" or "pilots" gave directions to the next stop. "Conductors" or "engineers" led the "passengers," "cargo," or "goods" on foot or by rowboat.

The conductors took fugitives down the "line" to "stations" or "depots" operated by "stationmasters." Coded messages about escapes were sent ahead to stationmasters, such as: "Look for those fleeces of wool by tomorrow."[10] The "cargo" was hidden in wagonloads of hay or vegetables, or in wagons built with false bottoms. Homes, schools, barns, and churches served as hiding places. People hid in cellars, attics, fake closets, secret rooms, and hand-dug tunnels connected to a main house. Minister John Rankin, a well-known conductor in Ohio, often left a light on in the upstairs window of his home to signal to runaways that it was safe to come inside.[11]

Fugitive slaves also wore disguises. Some carried tools to look as if they were going to work. Harriet Tubman fooled people by wearing fancy silk dresses that a slave would not own.[12]

Conductor John Fairfield helped a group of mixed-race passengers escape from Kentucky. He powdered their faces, gave them wigs, and passed them off as white. In 1848, one of the most famous escapes to freedom was by Ellen and William Craft, a slave couple who openly traveled to Philadelphia by train and steamboat. Ellen, with her light complexion, wore gentlemanly attire and posed as a man. Her husband, William, posed as her slave.[13]

Ellen and William Craft

CHAPTER 2

Levi Coffin: President of the Underground Railroad

The Bible, in bidding us to feed the hungry and clothe the naked, said nothing about color. . . . I was willing to receive and aid as many fugitives as were disposed to come to my house.[1]
—*Levi Coffin*

Levi Coffin, a white Quaker born in 1798 in North Carolina, and his wife, Catharine, provided food and shelter to fugitive slaves in Indiana and Ohio for thirty-three years. They helped more than three thousand slaves escape to freedom. Their busy home became known as the Grand Central Station of the Underground Railroad.

Levi's parents and grandparents strongly opposed slavery. Growing up in North Carolina exposed Levi to the mistreatment of slaves. At age seven he shockingly saw a slave with chains around his neck and his wrists handcuffed. The recaptured slave had been sold from his wife and children and chained to keep him from running back to see them. The slave was then brutally

Levi Coffin was called the "President of the Underground Railroad." He and his wife helped more than 3,000 runaways escape to freedom.

Catherine Coffin

tortured for refusing to give information about who helped him. Levi never forgot the cruel treatment he witnessed as a child and vowed to change things.[2]

Married in 1826, Levi and Catharine moved to Newport, Indiana. Levi opened a general store and became a successful businessman. Still, his most important duty was working for the Underground Railroad. The Coffins turned their eight-room redbrick house into a safe haven for fugitive slaves heading north to freedom.

Levi remembers during that first winter seeing runaway slaves hiding in the woods and thickets and waiting for their chance to obtain food and assistance. He wrote, "I would invite them, in a low tone, to come in, and they would follow me into the darkened house without a word, for we knew who might be watching and listening." Levi's basement was used as a hiding place. Once the runaways were escorted inside, the door was locked, a bed pushed in front of it, the windows covered, and a fire lit.[3]

Runaways arrived at their house from all areas of the South. Late at night a tap at the door often awakened Levi and Catharine. Outside they might find a two-horse wagon carrying two to seventeen fugitives. Catharine would fix a meal and prepare places for them to sleep. The passengers might stay with them for only one night, but if they were sick or too exhausted they stayed longer and received medical assistance.

Levi hitched a team of horses and a wagon to take runaways at night to the next depot. They traveled through muddy and rutted roads where people rarely traveled. Levi used every precaution on these dangerous journeys.

One night Levi received a message that slave catchers were trailing the seventeen fugitives in his house. The next morning he took the slaves in wagons on scattered routes, making it difficult for them to be found. When the slave catchers arrived, a friend of Levi's was posted at his door with two loaded pistols. The hunters hung around town for weeks, searching for the fugitives. They finally gave up, but before leaving town they passed the Coffin house and yelled: "There's an Underground Railroad around here and Levi Coffin is its president!"[4] Word soon spread about the incident and letters came to their house addressed to "Levi Coffin, President of the Underground Railroad."

Coffin's friends warned him that harboring runaways would ruin his business. Levi responded: "I told them that I felt no condemnation for anything that I had

The busy Coffin house became known as the "Grand Central Station of the Underground Railroad" because of the thousands of runaway slaves who passed through the Coffin's home while escaping their masters.

Levi Coffin used a wagon like this one to smuggle fugitive slaves. The wagons would bounce through the night along muddy and rugged roads to the next depot.

ever done for the fugitive slaves. If by doing my duty . . . I injured my business, then let my business go. As to my safety, my life was in the hands of my Divine Master, and I felt I had his approval."

Levi's business survived and prospered as the town grew. He became director of the local bank. The Coffins served as role models to the community in their efforts to help the fugitives. Many white families, though reluctant to take runaways into their homes, donated clothes and money to the cause.

The Coffins moved to Ohio in 1847. They remained committed to ending slavery and continued working as conductors on the Underground Railroad. Levi opened another store and refused to sell any goods that were made by slave labor.

Levi, Catharine, and their daughter toured Canada in 1854 and ran into many of the people they helped. "Hundreds who had been sheltered under our roof and fed at our table, when fleeing from the land of whips and chains, introduced themselves to us and referred to the time, often fifteen or twenty years before, when we had aided them."[5]

Harriet Beecher Stowe and *Uncle Tom's Cabin*

When Harriet Beecher Stowe wrote about the horrors of slavery, she had no idea her book would be so powerful. Her novel, *Uncle Tom's Cabin,* sold 300,000 copies in 1852.[6] It is still in print.

Harriet Elizabeth Beecher was born in Connecticut on June 14, 1811. Her family was devoted to social justice and antislavery causes. Her father was a dynamic religious leader. In 1836, Harriet married Calvin Ellis Stowe, a biblical scholar. The two supported the Underground Railroad and provided shelter to fugitive slaves.

The family moved to Maine in 1850 when Calvin Stowe began teaching at Bowdoin College. That year, the Fugitive Slave Law made it a crime to help runaway slaves, and free blacks could be returned to slavery. People in northern cities and free black communities panicked about their safety. They published stories and articles declaring their outrage.

Harriet Beecher Stowe

The characters in Stowe's novel were modeled after real people. Fugitive Eliza Harris, for example, nearly died as she crossed an icy Ohio River with her baby tucked in her arm. Josiah Henson (Uncle Tom) escaped to Canada on the Underground Railroad. He founded a town in Canada for former slaves to learn a trade and live independently.

Although modern critics view Stowe's black characters as stereotypical, her descriptions of the cruelties of slavery captured the nation's attention. Inspired readers supported the Underground Railroad and insisted that slavery be abolished.

CHAPTER 3

Frederick Douglass: Freedom Fighter

"My Dear Mrs. Post: Please shelter this Sister from the house of bondage till five o'clock—this afternoon—She will then be sent on to the land of freedom. Yours truly, Fred K."[1]
—Underground Railroad Pass written by Frederick Douglass

Frederick Douglass wanted to help passengers escape a life of servitude the same way he'd been helped. His home in Rochester, New York, was a station on the Underground Railroad. He and his wife, Anna Murray, clothed and fed hundreds of runaway slaves and assisted them on their journey to Canada.

Douglass was a gifted writer and powerful speaker. Tall and imposing, his beautiful speaking voice inspired audiences during his antislavery speeches. He fearlessly lectured crowds even when in danger of being kidnapped and sold back into slavery.

Frederick Douglass (circa 1818–1852) escaped slavery to become one of the greatest voices for freedom who ever lived.

William Lloyd Garrison, editor of the abolitionist journal *The Liberator*, was so impressed with Douglass, he invited him to speak at the Massachusetts Antislavery Society's annual convention. Garrison wrote:

I shall never forget his first speech at the convention . . . the extraordinary emotion it excited in my own mind . . . the powerful impression it created . . . the applause which followed from the beginning to the end . . . I think I never hated slavery so intensely as at that moment . . . there stood one, in physical proportion and stature commanding and exact . . . in intellect richly endowed . . . yet a slave, ay, a fugitive slave.[2]

William Lloyd Garrison helped form the American Anti-Slavery Society and later fought for the woman suffrage movement.

Douglass' writings were eloquent and influential. He published an antislavery newspaper called *The North Star.* Douglass called it that because the North Star's light guided fugitive slaves to the free states in the North.

Frederick Douglass was born Fredrick Augustus Bailey on a small plantation in Tuckahoe, Maryland. He decided that 1818 was the year of his birth after hearing his master say that he was seven years old in 1825.

Frederick was separated from his mother, Harriet Bailey, as an infant. She worked on a farm twelve miles away.

Frederick Douglass

Family members told him his father was a white man and possibly his master, but he was never sure. His grandparents, Isaac and Betsy, raised him. He became especially close to his grandmother, an expert at fishing and farming. In 1824, when Frederick was six, his grandmother took him on a long walk to the plantation of their master to work and left him there. Frederick was very hurt and found it hard to trust anyone after that.[3]

Frederick saw his mother only a few times in his life. His mother, a field hand, could be whipped for not showing up on the field at sunrise. Frederick wrote, "She was with me in the night. She would lie down with me, and get me to sleep, but long before I waked she was gone."[4] He never got the chance to really know his mother. She died when he was seven.

At eight, Frederick was sent to Baltimore to work for owner Thomas Auld's brother and sister-in-law, Hugh and Sophia. Sophia was a kind woman and taught him how to read and spell. But when Hugh found out, he ordered Sophia to stop, stating it was "unlawful" and "unsafe" to teach a slave to read. He argued it would spoil him, make him "discontented" and "unhappy" to be a slave, and "of no value to his master."[5]

Frederick realized that reading and writing formed the "pathway from slavery to freedom." He continued to learn secretly. He'd take bread from the kitchen to give to the poor white boys in the neighborhood, and they taught him how to read.

In 1833, Thomas Auld brought Frederick back to Maryland's Eastern Shore. He was sent to work in the field with Edward Covey, a poor white farmer known as a slave-breaker. Within a week Covey severely whipped

Mrs. Sophia Auld teaching young Frederick Douglass to read

him, "cutting my back, causing the blood to run, and raising ridges on my flesh as large as my little fingers." Covey regularly whipped the teenager until Frederick fought back. The slaves watching the battle refused to do anything when Covey cried for help. Covey never whipped Frederick again. Douglas recalled, "This battle with Mr. Covey . . . was the turning point in my life as a slave . . . I was nothing before; I was a man now!"[6]

Anna Murray

Douglass vowed to escape.

He failed in his first escape attempts. But in 1838, disguised in a sailor's uniform and carrying identification papers he received from a free black seaman, Douglass boarded a train to Maryland. He traveled openly, taking the ferry across the Susquehanna River at Havre de Grace, then a train to Wilmington, and a steamboat to Philadelphia. He arrived in New York by train within 24 hours of his escape from slavery.

"Frederick Douglass Appealing to President Lincoln and His Cabinet to Enlist Negroes" mural by William Edouard Scott

He was taken into the home of a supporter of the Railroad and kept well hidden until days later, when his fiancée, Anna Murray, joined him. They were married September 15, 1838, by a black abolitionist, Reverend James W. C. Pennington. They adopted Johnson as their married named and later changed it to Douglass.

Now a free man, Frederick Douglass became a great leader in the antislavery movement. He was a trusted adviser to Abraham Lincoln, a strong advocate for women's rights, and in his later years a Minister-General to the Republic of Haiti.

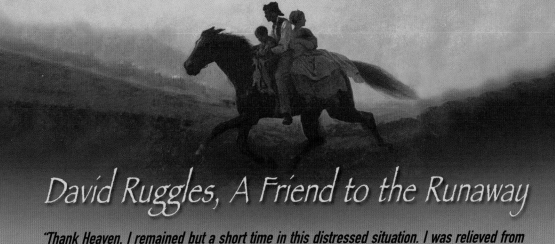

David Ruggles, A Friend to the Runaway

"Thank Heaven, I remained but a short time in this distressed situation. I was relieved from it by the humane hand of Mr. David Ruggles, whose vigilance, kindness, and perseverance, I shall never forget. I am glad of an opportunity to express, as far as words can, the love and gratitude I bear him." [1] —Frederick Douglass

When Frederick Douglass first arrived in New York, he was warned to beware of slave catchers and kidnappers. He didn't know whom to trust. A friend introduced him to David Ruggles, known for befriending runaways. Ruggles warmly greeted him and took him into the headquarters of the New York Committee of Vigilance. He helped Douglass craft his plans for the future. He even arranged for a minister and marriage ceremony for Douglass and his fiancée. Once Frederick was ready to begin a new life and leave for New England, Ruggles gave him money and a letter of introduction.

Born a free black man in Connecticut in 1810, David Ruggles moved to New York in 1827. He opened the first African American bookstore and wrote and published hundreds of antislavery pamphlets and articles, making him the first black publisher in the nation.[2] Ruggles was beaten by an angry mob and his bookstore destroyed, but he later reopened it.

Ruggles was involved in many antislavery organizations. As a conductor on the Underground Railroad, he helped over 600 slaves escape to freedom. He is best known for his work as secretary of the New York Committee of Vigilance. The committee helped runaway slaves adjust to daily life once they made it to freedom. It helped them adopt new identities; find homes and work; gave them money and letters of introduction; and taught them how to avoid slave catchers. It also convinced the government to grant jury trials for recaptured slaves and found lawyers for them.

David Ruggles

CHAPTER 4

William Still: Father of the Underground Railroad

"It was my good fortune to lend a helping hand to the weary travelers flying from the land of bondage."[1]
—*William Still*

William remembers his first time helping a slave escape from slave catchers. The only thing he regretted is he never knew the man's name. Years later, William played an important role in helping hundreds of slaves escape on the Underground Railroad to freedom. But that incident in his childhood also made him realize that their names and stories should never be forgotten.

William Still was born a free black man in 1821 in New Jersey. His parents were born into slavery, but his father, Levin Steel, purchased his freedom. Levin moved to New Jersey and was later joined by his wife, Charity, who escaped with their four children. But Charity and the children were recaptured and returned to the slave owner. She escaped successfully the second time with their two

Writer, historian, and one of the key leaders of the abolitionist movement, William Still was often called the "Father of the Underground Railroad." He helped hundreds of slaves to escape to freedom and kept detailed records of their lives.

daughters but was forced to leave their sons, Peter and Levy, behind. The master angrily sold the boys and they ended up in the Deep South in Alabama. Later, Levin changed his name to Still to protect his wife and family. They had fourteen more children, including William.

In 1844, William moved to Philadelphia, Pennsylvania. He had little formal education, but worked hard at teaching himself how to read and write. He married Letitia George in 1847 and worked as a clerk for the Pennsylvania Antislavery Society. He became secretary and chairman of the Vigilance Committee and one of the leaders of the abolitionist movement. During this time he worked as a stationmaster on the Underground Railroad. He helped runaway slaves traveling to Philadelphia.

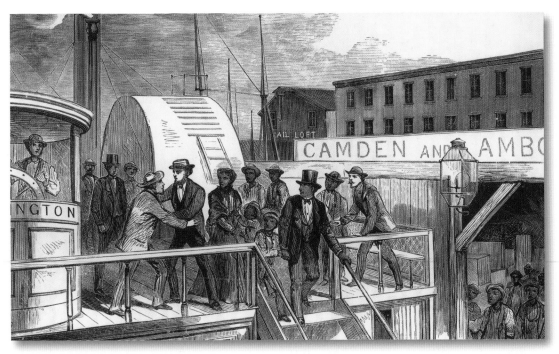

In 1855, slave owner John Wheeler passed through Philadelphia with his slave Jane Johnson. She was freed along with her children by William Still and other members of the Anti-Slavery Society. Still later faced a prison sentence but was found not guilty. He published this drawing of the rescue of Jane Johnson.

Still was chairman of the Vigilance Committee of the Pennsylvania Anti-Slavery Society. In 1872, he published *The Underground Railroad Records,* contained a collection of the interviews and secret notes he wrote while helping the slaves to freedom.

William worked with Underground Railroad agents throughout the South, New Jersey, New York, New England, and Canada. Harriet Tubman traveled through his network to freedom, and she also used his lines for her fugitive passengers. His activism earned William the title "Father of the Underground Railroad." Besides piloting hundreds of slaves to freedom, he wrote the first detailed account of the Underground Railroad.

At first he didn't write the fugitives' stories down, fearing for their safety. As he wrote in the book's introduction: "The risk of aiding fugitives was never lost sight of and the safety of all concerned called for still tongues. Sad and thrilling stories were listened to and made deep impressions; but as a universal rule, friend and fugitive parted with only very vivid recollection of the secret interview . . ."[2]

Despite the risks, William knew he was witnessing history and this information was too important to lose. He kept daily records and wrote the stories of the men

and women who traveled through the Philadelphia region on the Underground Railroad. In the book he published years later, William explained he owed it "to the cause of Freedom and to the Fugitives and their descendants to bring the doings of the Underground Railroad before the public in the most truthful manner...to show what efforts were made and what success was gained for freedom."

One of Still's most rewarding interviews took place with a former slave named Peter. The man told Still he'd been taken from his family at age six. After forty years he was finally able to buy his freedom, but unfortunately his brother Levy had died still a slave. After sharing more details about his parents and family, William was shocked but thrilled to discover that Peter was his brother!

William Still always made sure the recorded information was hidden and safe. After the Civil War, his interviews were finally made public. In 1872, Still published his groundbreaking historical diary, *The Underground Railroad: A Record of Facts, Authentic Narratives, Letters, etc., Narrating the Hardships, Hairbreadth Escapes, and Death Struggles of the Slaves in their efforts for Freedom as Related by Themselves and Others, or Witnessed by the Author.*

Still prospered in business and became a well-known leader in Philadelphia's black community. He successfully campaigned to end segregation on Philadelphia's trolley cars, started a black-owned savings and loan, established an orphanage for black youth, and organized the first YMCA for African Americans.[3]

Peter Still

The Fugitive Slave Act of 1850

Thousands of escaped slaves found freedom in the Northern states, Canada, Mexico, the Caribbean, and among Native Americans. Southern newspapers published notices from furious slave owners seeking runaways. They demanded stronger penalties for anyone who violated the 1793 Fugitive Slave Act.

This act gave law enforcement officers and private citizens the right to seize fugitive slaves and return them to their owners. Slave catchers were paid for returned escapees. Often using bloodhounds, they traveled along roads, rivers, and through the woods searching for runaways.[4] They didn't care if they caught the right person. They forced people to "confess" they belonged to a certain owner by whipping them or throwing them into dungeons.

Many people in the free states ignored these laws. Since the Northern states were in the process of abolishing slavery, slaves had more places to flee.

Congress passed the Fugitive Slave Act of 1850, a much tougher law expanding the rights of slaveholders. All U.S. citizens were *required* to help slave catchers return escaped slaves to bondage, no matter how long a person had been free. The law made it a crime to help fugitive slaves.

It was a terrifying time for free blacks, runaways, and abolitionists. Thomas Sims, who lived in Boston, was the first fugitive arrested under the new law. He was returned by ship to Georgia, publicly whipped, and imprisoned for months before being sold. In Philadelphia, Thomas Hall and his wife were beaten and enslaved.

Calvin Fairbanks had led numerous slaves from the South to freedom. In 1852 he was caught and sentenced to fifteen years in prison. The guards tortured and beat him.[5] After five years the governor pardoned him. He resumed working as a conductor on the Underground Railroad.

Calvin Fairbanks

CHAPTER 5

Workers on the Underground Railroad

Most of the people who worked on the Underground Railroad were not famous, but all were heroes. They risked their lives for the cause of freedom. The workers came from different races, occupations, and all walks of life.

James Cummichael was a slave that cleverly rescued his wife from a well-guarded Louisiana-bound ship. He used the little money he earned to buy liquor for the ship's crew. Joking and playing games with them, James got the crewmembers so drunk they all fell asleep. He snuck his wife and other slaves off the boat and fled North to freedom.[1]

John Mason, a fugitive from Kentucky, returned and led over 1,300 slaves to freedom. On one raid, vicious dogs attacked them. Mason fought until both his arms were broken and the dogs had ripped his body. He was sold back into slavery, but later escaped to freedom in Canada.

This chapter briefly highlights other valiant people who risked their lives working on the Underground Railroad.

The letters *S.S.*, for slave stealer, can be seen branded on a hand in this photograph. It is the hand of Captain Jonathan W. Walker, one of many heroic people who would play a key role in the story of the Underground Railroad.

Thomas Garrett

Born in 1789 in Pennsylvania, Thomas Garrett, a Quaker and key Station Master for the Underground Railroad, helped more than 2,700 slaves escape.

In 1848, Garrett was arrested and convicted for breaking the Fugitive Slave Law. He was forced to sell all his properties to pay the fine. Bankrupt, yet defiant, Garrett told the court: "Judge, thou hast not left me a dollar, but I wish to say to thee, and to all in this courtroom, that if any one knows of a fugitive who wants a shelter and a friend, send him to Thomas Garrett and he will befriend him."[2]

Thomas Garrett

Samuel Burris

Born a free man in Delaware in 1808, Samuel Burris moved to Pennsylvania with his wife and children and became a member of the Pennsylvania Antislavery Society. In 1847, he was caught helping runaways. He was tried, convicted, and sentenced to be sold into slavery.

As Samuel stood nervously on the auction block, a man examined him and outbid the other slave traders. Once he was led away, Samuel was greatly relieved to hear the man whisper: "You have been bought with abolition gold."[3] The Pennsylvania Antislavery Society had secretly organized Samuel's purchase and rescue.

Samuel Burris

Jonathan Walker

In 1844, Captain Jonathan Walker, an antislavery supporter, attempted to take seven runaways by boat from Florida to the Bahamas. Walker and the fugitives were stopped and seized by bounty hunters. He was thrown in jail and "fastened to a ringbolt for fifteen days without bed or chair" while people threw eggs at him.

Jonathan Walker

Walker was convicted of stealing slaves, sentenced to solitary confinement, and ordered to carry forever the mark of "slave stealer." In a packed courtroom, a U.S. Marshal burned the letters SS into Walkers right palm with a hot branding iron.[4]

Abolitionists paid Walker's court costs and fines, and he was released from prison. He lectured throughout the country for years, proudly holding up his hand and showing audiences the mark he suffered for his beliefs. Walker's fellow antislavery activists said the SS in their eyes stood for "slave savior."[5]

John Fairfield

John Fairfield

John Fairfield was born in Virginia to a family that owned slaves and he hated it. As a young man he decided to live in Ohio, but first he helped his childhood friend, owned by his uncle, to escape to Canada. Thereafter, former slaves brought him their savings and begged him to bring their relatives back to freedom, too.

During the 1850s Fairfield established himself as one of the most passionate, cunning, and resourceful conductors on the Underground Railroad. He'd hang out in an area for months, planning with slaves and posing as a slaveholder or trader to gain the confidence and friendship of whites. This made it easier for him to lead their slaves away to freedom. Fairfield is said to have freed several thousand slaves. It is believed he was later killed in a slave revolt in Tennessee.[6]

John P. Parker

Born into slavery in Virginia in 1827, John Parker was the son of a slave mother and white father. At the age of eight he was sold to a doctor in Alabama. The doctor's family taught Parker to read and write, and he apprenticed at the local iron foundry.[7] Parker paid for his freedom with the money he saved from his apprenticeship.

John moved back to Ohio and in 1853 built a foundry behind his house. He became one of the few African Americans in the nineteenth century to obtain a U.S. patent. Parker actively worked on the Underground Railroad and in one of his most daring escapades not only rescued a slave couple on a plantation, but also snatched their baby from their master's bedside where the master slept with a lighted candle and loaded pistol. Shots rang out when the fugitives were halfway across the river, but Parker rowed hard and fast and got the couple and baby to safety.

John P. Parker's design for a soil pulverizer

Robert Purvis

Robert Purvis

One of the founders of the American Antislavery Society, Robert Purvis was born in Charleston, South Carolina in 1810, to a wealthy English merchant and a woman of German-Jewish and African heritage.[8] Although Robert's skin was light enough to pass for white, he viewed himself as black. His father, an outspoken abolitionist, moved the family to Philadelphia in 1819. When he died Robert inherited a large sum of money that he successfully invested in real estate.

Robert used his education and resources to fight slavery. A mentor and father figure to him was James Forten, a noted African American businessman. Robert married his daughter, Harriet, and they became involved in the abolitionist movement. Their home in Philadelphia became a way station for runaway slaves heading to Canada. The Purvises provided shelter to thousands of fugitives. Angry white mobs often vandalized their home because they thought Robert was a white man married to a black woman.[9]

"Friends" of the Underground Railroad

There were many people who worked as "friends" of the Underground Railroad. They fought against inequality from the pulpit, podium, and pen.

Frances Ellen Watkins Harper

Frances Ellen Watkins Harper: Harper was born in Baltimore in 1825 to free African American parents. After teaching in Ohio and Pennsylvania, she helped slaves escape through the Underground Railroad, and those "passengers" became the subject of her poems. Harper earned the title "Mother of African American journalism."[10] She lectured to large audiences about civil rights, women's rights, education, and the need to boycott slave labor.

William Lloyd Garrison: A founding member of the American Anti-Slavery Society, Garrison was born in Massachusetts in 1805. He argued for slaves to be freed and for them to receive citizenship.[11] In the first issue of his fiery newspaper *The Liberator*, Garrison wrote: "On this subject [slavery], I do not wish to think, or speak, or write with moderation . . . I will not excuse . . . I will not retreat a single inch . . . AND I WILL BE HEARD!"[12]

David Walker: The son of a slave father and free black mother, David Walker was born in 1796 in North Carolina. As a child he witnessed a slave forced to beat his mother until she died. He later moved to Boston. By 1828 he had become one of Boston's leading antislavery activists. He wrote and published a pamphlet called *The Appeal*, aimed at the enslaved people of the South.

 The Appeal challenged racism and urged slaves to rebel against their masters. Outraged slave owners posted a $10,000 reward for Walker's capture and $1,000 to kill him.[13] Supporters of the Underground Railroad promised to help Walker flee to Canada. He refused, saying: "Somebody must die in this cause. . . . I may be doomed . . . but it is not in me to falter if I can promote the work of emancipation."[14]

CONCLUSION

John Brown's Holy War

"When I think how he gave up his life for our people . . . it's clear to me it wasn't mortal man, it was God in him . . ."[1]

—Harriet Tubman on the death of John Brown

John Brown wearily stepped back inside his home. He grabbed one of his Sharpe rifles and eased back into his rocking chair. He opened his Bible again and resumed reading his favorite passages.

Brown often fed, clothed, and helped blacks fleeing from bondage to get from one station to another. He also strongly felt it was his God-given duty to protect them from physical harm. Many conductors were pacifists, but he was willing to shoot if necessary.

Brown became impatient with all the "talk," and like David Walker, believed an armed invasion of the South was the only true way to end slavery. Many abolitionists disagreed with his tactics, warning him it could end in his death. But Brown didn't care. He believed he was a messenger from God and this was his "Holy War."

Brown staged his course when he moved his family to Kansas in 1855. There he became even more involved in the antislavery movement. He hoped that Kansas would join the Union as a free state.[2] His passions and activity in the antislavery movement escalated to violence in 1856. Brown and his followers killed a group of proslavery supporters.

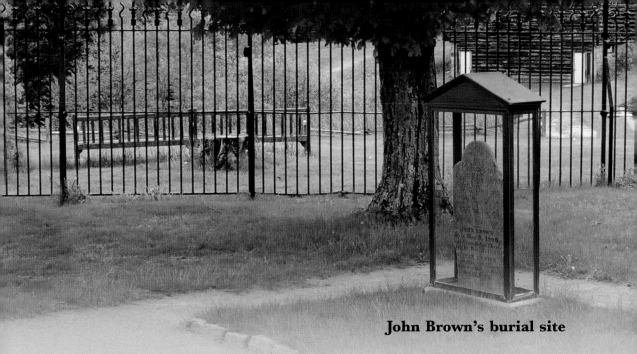

John Brown's burial site

In 1859 Brown led a small army of 21 men on a raid to capture weapons and munitions from the federal arsenal at Harpers Ferry, Virginia. Brown's strategy was to arm slaves with the weapons they seized and lead a revolt. His plan failed, and his men were either killed or captured. Brown was tried and convicted of treason. Before sentencing, Brown was allowed to make a statement to the court:

"I believe that to have interfered as I have done, as I have always freely admitted I have done in behalf of His despised poor, is no wrong, but right. Now, if it is deemed necessary that I should forfeit my life in the furtherance of the ends of justice, and mingle my blood further with the blood of my children and with the blood of millions in this slave country whose rights are disregarded by wicked, cruel, and unjust enactments . . . I say let it be done!"[3]

On the final day of his life, December 2, 1859, John Brown walked slowly and unflinchingly to the gallows. He handed a note to one of his jailers before he was hanged. The note was one more blast of the trumpet from him for the antislavery movement. It read: "I, John Brown, am now quite certain that the crimes of this guilty land will never be purged away but with blood."[4]

John Brown did not die in vain. His martyrdom inspired many people worldwide. Some historians believe his death sparked the American Civil War, which began less than two years later.

1619   Slavery in America begins when the first African slaves are brought to Jamestown, Virginia, to work on tobacco plantations.

1663   The first recorded slave rebellion takes place in Gloucester County, Virginia.

1773   Phillis Wheatley publishes *Poems on Various Subjects, Religious and Moral*. Her book is considered the first to be written by an African-American woman.

1775   Five thousand African-American men serve in the Revolutionary War.

1793   The U.S. Congress passes the first Fugitive Slave Law.

1820   The Missouri Compromise allows Missouri to enter the Union as a slave state, but makes slavery illegal in Maine. It prohibits slavery above the 36° 30´ latitude line in the rest of the Louisiana Territory.

1831   William Lloyd Garrison prints the first edition of *The Liberator*. In Nat Turner's slave rebellion, 55 whites are killed.

1838   Frederick Bailey escapes enslavement in Baltimore and finds freedom and a new name—Frederick Douglass—in Massachusetts.

1839   Harriet Tubman escapes to freedom. She returns to the south 19 times and leads hundreds of people north.

1849   Henry Box Brown is shipped to freedom in Pennsylvania.

1850   The Fugitive Slave Law is passed, making it illegal to help runaways in any manner.

1854   The Kansas-Nebraska Act repeals the Missouri Compromise.

1857   In the Dred Scott Decision, the U.S. Supreme Court rules that slaves are not considered people under the U.S. Constitution but are the property of their owners.

1859   John Brown raids Harpers Ferry, Virginia, for weapons to lead a slave revolt. He is captured and hanged.

1861   The Civil War begins.

1863   On January 1, Abraham Lincoln's Emancipation Proclamation frees all slaves in the Confederate States.

1865   The Civil War ends. All slaves in the United States are declared free. Texas hears the news on June 16, a holiday still celebrated as Juneteenth.

1868   The 14th Amendment grants citizenship to "all persons born or naturalized in the United States," including former slaves.

1870   The 15th Amendment grants African-American men the right to vote.

1872   William Still publishes *The Underground Railroad Records*.

CHAPTER NOTES

Introduction: The Avenging Angel

1. Ron Field, *Avenging Angel: John Brown's Raid on Harpers Ferry 1859* (Oxford: Osprey Publishing, 2012), p. 75.

2. David S. Reynolds, *John Brown, Abolitionist: The Man Who Killed Slavery, Sparked the Civil War; And Seeded Civil Rights* (New York: Alfred A. Knopf, 2005), p. 122.

3. The Library of Congress, "Elijah Lovejoy," *American Memory,* http://memory.loc.gov/ammem/today/nov07.html

4. Reynolds, pp. 129–130.

5. Michele Bollinger and Dao X. Tran, eds., *101 Changemakers: Rebels and Radicals Who Changed U.S. History* (Chicago: Haymarket Books, 2012), p. 23.

Chapter One

1. Reginald F. Davis, *Frederick Douglass: A Precursor of Liberation Theology* (Macon, Georgia: Mercer University Press, 2005), p. 63.

2. Amy Alexander, *Fifty Black Women Who Changed America* (New York: Kensington Publishing Corp., 1999), p. 19.

3. Sarah Bradford, *Harriet Tubman: The Moses of Her People.* (Mineola: Dover Publications, 2004), pp. 17–18.

4. Beverly Lowry, *Harriet Tubman: Imagining a Life* (New York: First Anchor Books, 2007), pp. 151–152.

5. United States *History: Underground Railroad,* http://www.u-s-history.com/pages/h481.html

6. Henrietta Buckmaster, *Let My People Go: The Story of the Underground Railroad and the Growth of the Abolition Movement* (Columbia: University of South Carolina, 1992), p. 215.

7. James A. McGowan and William C. Kashatus, *Harriet Tubman: A Biography* (Santa Barbara: Greenwood, 2011), p. 72.

8. David W. Blight, ed., *The Underground Railroad In History and Memory: Passages to Freedom* (Washington: Smithsonian, 2004), p. 201.

9. William Still, *The Underground Railroad: A Record of Facts, Authentic Narrative, Letters, &c.* (Philadelphia: Porter & Coates, 1872), http://www.gutenberg.org/files/15263/15263-h/15263-h.htm

10. William Lewis Nida, *The Story of Illinois and Its People* (Chicago: O. P. Barnes, 1913), p. 213, https://archive.org/stream/storyofillinoisi00nida#page/212/mode/2up

11. Raymond Bial, *The Underground Railroad* (Boston: Houghton Mifflin Company, 1995), p. 29.

12. Kate Clifford Larson, "Bound For the Promised Land: Harriet Tubman, Portrait of an American Hero," http://www.harriettubmanbiography.com/harriet-tubman-s-flight-to-freedom.html

13. Betty Deramus, *Forbidden Fruit: Love Stories From The Underground Railroad* (New York: Atria Books, 2005), pp. 41–45.

Chapter Two

1. Robert Felgar, *American Slavery: A Historical Exploration of Literature* (Santa Barbara: Greenwood, 2015), p. 76.

2. George and Willene Hendrick, eds., *Stories of The Underground Railroad As Told by Levi Coffin and William Still* (Chicago: Ivan R. Dee, 2004), pp. 35–45.

3. Bial, pp. 30–31.

4. Buckmaster, pp. 78–79.

5. Coffin, *Reminiscences,* p. 150.

6. Uncle Tom's Cabin—The Harriet Beecher Stowe Center. https://www.harrietbeecherstowecenter.org/utc/

Chapter Three

1. Bial, p. 38.

2. Frederick Douglass, *Narrative of the Life of Frederick Douglass, An American Slave Written by Himself* (New Haven: Yale University Press, 2001) p. 3.

3. William S. McFeely, *Frederick Douglass* (New York: Simon & Schuster, 1991).

4. Douglass, p. 14.

5. Ibid., 31.

6. McFeely, pp. 46–48

7. Douglass. p. 75.

8. The David Ruggles Center: http://www.davidrugglescenter.org/?page_id=7.

41

Chapter Four

1. Underground Railroad: The William Still Story, http://www.pbs.org/black-culture/shows/list/underground-railroad/home/

2. William Still, *The Underground Railroad: Authentic Narratives and First-Hand Accounts, Edited and with an Introduction by Ian Frederick Finseth* (Mineola, NY: Dover Publications, 2007), p. xvi.

3. Dr. Diane D. Turner, "William Still's National Significance," http://stillfamily.library.temple.edu/historical-perspective/william-still-significance

4. Bial, pp. 14–15.

5. Wilbur Henry Siebert, *The Underground Railroad From Slavery to Freedom* (New York: The Macmillan Company, 1899), p. 159.

Chapter Five

1. Buckmaster, p. 76.

2. Brian Temple, *Philadelphia Quakers and the Antislavery Movement* (Jefferson, NC: McFarland & Company, 2014), p. 166.

3. Don Papson and Tom Calarco, *Underground Railroad in New York City: Sydney Howard Gay, Louis Napoleon and the Record of Fugitives* (Jefferson, NC: McFarland & Company, Inc., 2015), p. 165.

4. Alvin F. Oickle, *The Man with the Branded Hand: The Life of Jonathan Walker, Abolitionist* (Yardley: Westholme Publishing, 2011), pp. 124–126.

5. W.M. Harford, Frank Edward Kittredge, and Parker Pillsbury, *The Man With The Branded Hand or a Short Sketch Of The Life And Services Of Jonathan Walker* (Muskegon, MI: Chronicle Steam Printing House, 1879), p. 20.

6. Buckmaster, pp. 194–197.

7. John P. Parker, http://www.nps.gov/nr/travel/underground/oh2.htm.

8. Faith Berry, ed., *From Bondage To Liberation: Writings by and about Afro-Americans from 1700-1918,* (New York: The Continuum International Publishing Group, 2006), p. 227.

9. Robert Purvis: http://usslave.blogspot.com/2012/07/african-american-abolitionist-named.html.

10. Frances Ellen Watkins Harper, http://www.poetryfoundation.org/bio/frances-ellen-watkins-harper.

11. Joseph R. Conlin, *The American Past: A Survey of American History* (Boston: Cengage Learning, 2010), p. 297.

12. William Lloyd Garrison—Liberator: "To the Public," http://www.pbs.org/wgbh/aia/part4/4h2928t.html

13. Buckmaster, p. 43.

14. David Walker (PBS), http://www.pbs.org/wgbh/aia/part4/4p2930.html

Conclusion: John Brown's Holy War

1. Jean M. Humez, *Harriet Tubman: The Life and the Life Stories* (Madison: The University of Wisconsin Press, 2004), p. 40.

2. Jacqueline L. Tobin, *From Midnight To Dawn: The Last Tracks Of The Underground Railroad* (New York: Doubleday, 2007), p. 47.

3. Robert E. McGlone, *John Brown's War Against Slavery* (New York: Cambridge University Press, 2009), pp. 315–316.

4. "John Brown," *Civil War Trust,* http://www.civilwar.org/education/history/biographies/john-brown.html

Books

Adler, David A. *Harriet Tubman and the Underground Railroad*. New York: Holiday House, 2013.

Blockson, Charles L. *The Underground Railroad: First-Person Narratives of Escapes to Freedom in the North*. New York: Prentice Hall Press, 1987.

Calarco, Tom. *Places of the Underground Railroad: A Geographical Guide*. Santa Barbara: Greenwood, 2011.

Hansen, Joyce, and Gary McGowan. F*reedom Roads: Searching for the Underground Railroad*. Chicago: Cricket Books, 2003

Hodges, Graham Russell. *David Ruggles: A Radical Black Abolitionist and the Underground Railroad in New York City*. Chapel Hill: University of North Carolina Press, 2010.

Landau, Elaine. *Fleeing to Freedom on the Underground Railroad: The Courageous Slaves, Agents, and Conductors*. Minneapolis: Twenty-First Century Books, 2006.

Sawyer, Kem Knapp. *The Underground Railroad in American History*. Springfield: Enslow Publishers, Inc., 1997.

Walker, Sally M. *Freedom Song: The Story of Henry "Box" Brown*. New York: HarperCollins, 2012.

Williams, Carla. *The Underground Railroad*. Chanhassen: The Child's World 2002.

Works Consulted

Alexander, Amy. *Fifty Black Women Who Changed America*. New York: Kensington Publishing Corp., 1999.

Berry, Faith, ed. *From Bondage to Liberation: Writings by and about Afro-Americans from 1700–1918*. New York: The Continuum International Publishing Group, 2006.

Bial, Raymond. *The Underground Railroad*. Boston: Houghton Mifflin Company, 1995.

Blight, David W., ed., *The Underground Railroad In History And Memory: Passages To Freedom*. Washington: Smithsonian, 2004.

Bollinger, Michele, and Dao X. Tran, eds. *101 Changemakers: Rebels and Radicals Who Changed US History*. Chicago: Haymarket Books, 2012.

Bradford, Sarah. *Harriet Tubman: The Moses of Her People*. Mineola: Dover Publications, 2004.

Buckmaster, Henrietta. *Let My People Go: The Story of the Underground Railroad and the Growth of the Abolition Movement*. Columbia: University of South Carolina Press, 1992.

Carbado, Devon W., and Donald Weise, eds. *The Long Walk to Freedom*. Boston: Beacon Press, 2012.

Coffin, Levi. *Reminiscences of Levi Coffin the Reputed President of the Underground Railroad.* Cincinnati: Robert Clarke & Co., 1880.

Conlin, Joseph R. *The American Past: A Survey of American History.* Boston: Cengage Learning, 2010.

Davis, Reginald F. *Frederick Douglass: A Precursor of Liberation Theology.* Macon, GA: Mercer University Press, 2005.

DeRamus, Betty. *Forbidden Fruit: Love Stories From the Underground Railroad.* New York: Atria Books, 2005.

Douglass, Frederick. *Narrative of Frederick Douglass, An American Slave Written by Himself.* New Haven: Yale University Press, 2001.

Felgar, Robert. *American Slavery: A Historical Exploration of Literature.* Santa Barbara: Greenwood, 2015.

Field, Ron, *Avenging Angel: John Brown's Raid on Harpers Ferry 1859.* Oxford: Osprey Publishing, 2012.

Harford, W.M., Frank Edward Kittredge, and Parker Pillsbury. *The Man With The Branded Hand or a Short Sketch Of The Life And Services Of Jonathan Walker.* Muskegon, MI: Chronicle Steam Printing House, 1879.

Hedrick, Joan D. *Harriet Beecher Stowe: A Life.* New York: Oxford University Press, 1994.

Hendrick, George and Willene, eds. *Stories Of The Underground Railroad As Told by Levi Coffin and William Still.* Chicago: Ivan R. Dee 2004.

Humez, Jean M. *Harriet Tubman: The Life and the Life Stories.* Madison: The University of Wisconsin Press.

Larson, Kate Clifford. "Bound For the Promised Land: Harriet Tubman, Portrait of an American Hero." http://www.harriettubmanbiography.com/harriet-tubman-s-flight-to-freedom.html

Lewis, David Levering. *W.E.B. Du Bois: Biography of a Race.* New York: Henry Holt and Company, 1993.

Lowry, Beverly. *Harriet Tubman: Imagining A Life.* New York: First Anchor Books, 2007.

McFeely, William S. *Frederick Douglass.* New York: Simon & Schuster, 1991.

McGlone, Robert E. *John Brown's War Against Slavery.* New York: Cambridge University Press, 2009.

McGowan, James A., and William C. Kashatus. *Harriet Tubman: A Biography.* Santa Barbara: Greenwood, 2011.

Oickle, Alvin F. *The Man With The Branded Hand: The Life of Jonathan Walker; Abolitionist.* Yardley, PA: Westholme Publishing, 2011.

FURTHER READING

Papson, Don, and Tom Calarco. *Underground Railroad in New York City: Sydney Howard Gay, Louis Napoleon and the Record of Fugitives.* Jefferson, NC: McFarland & Company, Inc., 2015.

Reynolds, David S. *John Brown, Abolitionist: The Man Who Killed Slavery, Sparked the Civil War; And Seeded Civil Rights.* New York: Alfred A. Knopf, 2005.

Siebert, Wilbur Henry. *The Underground Railroad From Slavery to Freedom.* New York: The Macmillan Company, 1899.

Still, William. *The Underground Railroad: Authentic Narratives and First-Hand Accounts. Edited and with an Introduction by Ian Frederick Finseth.* Mineola, NY: Dover Publications, 2007.

Temple, Brian. *Philadelphia Quakers and the Antislavery Movement.* Jefferson, NC: McFarland & Company, 2014.

Tobin, Jacqueline L. *From Midnight To Dawn: The Last Tracks Of The Underground Railroad.* New York: Doubleday, 2007.

On the Internet

David Walker Biography:
   http://docsouth.unc.edu/nc/walker/bio.html
Harriet Tubman:
   http://www.nyhistory.com/harriettubman/life.htm
Henry "Box" Brown Biography:
   http://www.spartacus.schoolnet.co.uk/USASbox.htm
John Brown Farm and Gravesite:
   http://www.nps.gov/nr/travel/underground/ny4.htm
John P. Parker Biography:
   http://www.ohiohistorycentral.org/w/John_P._Parker
Levi Coffin House:
   http://www.waynet.org/levicoffin/
"Operating the Underground Railroad":
   http://www.nps.gov/nr/travel/underground/opugrr.htm
Thomas Garrett Biography:
   http://www.russpickett.com/history/garrbio.htm
"William Lloyd Garrison and *The Liberator*"
   http://www.ushistory.org/us/28a.asp

GLOSSARY

abolitionist (ab-oh-LIH-shuh-nist)—A person who wanted to outlaw slavery in the United States.

auction (AWK-shun)—A public sale of goods or property to the highest bidder.

avenging (uh-VEN-jing)—Harming someone who has harmed others.

bondage (BON-dij)—The state of being a slave.

brand—To permanently mark an animal or person with a hot iron.

code—A system of words, figures, or other symbols that replace other words for the purpose of secrecy.

convict (kun-VIKT)—To find a person guilty of a crime.

editor (ED-ih-ter)—A person who decides the final content of a newspaper, book, magazine, or other publication.

emancipation (ee-man-sih-PAY-shun)—Freedom from slavery.

forfeit (FOR-fit)—To give up property or rights as a penalty for doing wrong.

fugitive (FYOO-jih-tiv)—A person who flees or escapes from a place or is in hiding.

haven (HAY-ven)—A place of safety.

heritage (HAYR-ih-tij)—Something handed down through a family.

illiterate (il-IH-tuh-rit)—Not able to read or write.

influential (in-floo-ENT-shul)—Able to change people's minds.

liberator (LIH-ber-ay-ter)—A person or tool that sets someone free.

martyrdom (MAR-ter-dum)—The decision to suffer and die on behalf of one's beliefs.

movement (MOOV-munt)—An organized effort to make a set of political, social, or artistic ideas a reality.

overseer (OH-ver-see-er)—A person who watches and directs the work of other people to make sure the job is done.

plantation (plan-TAY-shun)—A large estate or farm on which crops are raised.

rebellion (ree-BEL-yun)—A violent act of resistance against a government or authority.

stereotypical (stayr-ee-oh-TIH-pih-kul)—Having or claiming qualities that are usually falsely or unfairly believed to belong to an entire group.

treason (TREE-zun)—The crime of betraying one's country.

vigilance (VIH-juh-lintz)—A careful watch for possible danger.

PHOTO CREDITS: Pp. 6, 11, 13, 19, 21, 22, 34—Public Domain; p. 18—Christa Sterken; p. 24—Library of Congress; p. 36—nps.gov; pp. 7, 38–39—Tony Fischer. All other photos—CreativeCommons. Every measure has been taken to find all copyright holders of material used in this book. In the event any mistakes or omissions have happened within, attempts to correct them will be made in future editions of the book.